All you need to know about Venezuela

4

Introduction

The Republic of Venezuela, located in the northern part of South America, is a country of remarkable diversity and contrasts. With an area of about 916,445 square kilometers and a population of over 31 million people, Venezuela is a major player on the South American continent. The capital of the country is Caracas, which is also the economic and cultural center.

Geographically, Venezuela is extremely diverse. In the north, a long coastline stretches along the Caribbean Sea, known not only for its beautiful beaches, but also for its rich maritime biodiversity. The country is bordered by Colombia to the west, Brazil to the south, and Guyana to the east. Venezuela is also home to many unique geographical features, including the Orinoco River, one of the largest rivers in South America, and the world's tallest waterfall, Angel Falls.

Venezuela's history is marked by a complex sequence of political and social events. Before the arrival of the European conquerors, the country was home to various indigenous peoples, including the Caribs, the Arawak, and the Timoto-Cuicas. With the arrival of the Spanish in the 16th century, the colonial era began, which lasted for almost three centuries and left deep cultural and social traces. In the 19th century, the struggle for independence led by Simón Bolívar and other national heroes led to the founding of the Republic of Venezuela in 1811.

Venezuela's rich cultural tradition is reflected in its art, literature, music, and folklore. Famous Venezuelan artists such as Armando Reverón and Jesús Rafael Soto have gained international fame, while the Venezuelan music scene spans a variety of genres, from traditional joropo to modern styles such as salsa and reggaeton.

Venezuela's economy is largely shaped by its oil industry, which is one of the largest in the world. Oil accounts for a significant part of exports and has contributed to both economic development and social challenges in the country. Recently, Venezuela has faced political tensions and economic challenges that have led to a profound social crisis.

In the coming chapters, we will explore the diverse aspects of this fascinating country in more detail, from its rich wildlife and cuisine to its most significant tourist attractions and historic towns. Venezuela is a country with a complex and fascinating history that, despite its challenges, has preserved a rich cultural and natural heritage.

Geography and natural resources

Venezuela, a country of exceptional geographical diversity, covers an area of about 916,445 square kilometers in the northern part of South America. It borders Colombia to the west, Brazil to the south and Guyana to the east. The northern border is formed by the coast along the Caribbean Sea, which stretches for around 2800 kilometers and is one of the most beautiful in the world with its white sandy beaches and turquoise blue waters.

The geographical structure of Venezuela is extremely varied. In the north, the coastal plains stretch, while in the center of the country the Orinoco Basin spreads. One of the largest rivers in South America, the Orinoco River runs through the country for more than 2000 kilometers and drains a vast area that includes rainforests, savannahs and tropical wetlands.

In the south of Venezuela stretch the extensive foothills of the Amazon rainforest, which is home to incredible biodiversity and is considered the lungs of the planet. This part of the country is characterized by a tropical climate and provides habitat for a variety of animal and plant species, including rare species such as jaguars, tapirs, and macaws.

To the northwest rise the majestic Andes, which stretch across the countries of South America and reach heights of over 5000 meters in Venezuela. This mountain range is known not only for its scenic beauty, but also for its rich biodiversity and cultural significance for the indigenous peoples who live in the mountains.

The geological structure of Venezuela is complex and rich in natural resources. The country has extensive oil and natural gas reserves, which play a significant role in the national economy. These resources have made Venezuela one of the world's leading oil exporters, with the oil industry contributing to both economic development and social challenges.

In addition to its rich mineral resources such as iron ore, bauxite, and gold, Venezuela is also known for its gemstones, including the famous Venezuelan emerald. The diversity of natural resources is also reflected in agriculture, with coffee, cocoa, sugar cane and bananas being important export products.

Venezuela's geographical diversity makes it a unique destination for ecotourism and adventure travel. National parks such as Canaima National Park, home to Angel Falls, attract visitors from all over the world who want to experience the unspoiled nature and spectacular landscapes that Venezuela has to offer.

Historical Roots of Venezuela

Venezuela's historical roots date far back to the pre-Columbian era, when the area was inhabited by various indigenous peoples. Among these, the Caribs were present in the north, the Arawak in the west and the Timoto-Cuicas in the Andean regions. These peoples lived in different ecological zones, from the coast to the plains to the mountains, and each developed their own cultural and linguistic traditions.

The arrival of the European conquerors in the 15th century, led by Christopher Columbus, marked a turning point in Venezuela's history. The Spanish began to conquer and colonize the country, which offered rich mineral resources and a strategic location. Francisco de Orellana was one of the first Spanish explorers to explore the Orinoco River, and the colonial rulers established numerous settlements along the coast and inland.

In the 16th century, Venezuela became part of the Spanish Viceroyalty of Peru and later part of the Spanish headquarters in Caracas. Colonial rule was characterized by economic exploitation and social inequalities, as the indigenous population was enslaved and forced to work in mines and plantations. This period left deep social and cultural marks, while at the same time resistance to Spanish rule was forming.

In the late 18th and early 19th centuries, the desire for independence from the Spanish crown grew. Leaders such as Simón Bolívar and Francisco de Miranda led the independence movements, which led to several uprisings and wars. The struggle for liberation from Spanish colonialism reached its climax with Venezuela's declaration of independence on July 5, 1811 in Caracas.

After a long and turbulent period of wars of independence, Venezuela established itself as an independent republic. However, political instability and social tensions persisted, and the country faced internal power struggles, economic crises, and external interference that affected its development.

Venezuela's historical roots are deeply rooted in the struggles and successes of its indigenous peoples, colonial oppression, and the quest for independence. These complex and often contradictory events have shaped modern Venezuela, influencing its cultural diversity and its search for a stable and prosperous future.

Pre-Columbian cultures

Venezuela's pre-Columbian cultures were extremely diverse, developing over thousands of years in different ecological and geographical regions of the country. The earliest traces of human settlement date back to around 15,000 BC, when nomadic hunter-gatherers began to roam the area. Later, these nomadic groups developed into sedentary communities that practiced agriculture and founded the first permanent settlements.

The Caribs were one of the most important indigenous groups in Venezuela and inhabited mainly the coastal regions in the north of the country. They were known for their art of war and their social organization, which was strongly hierarchical. The Arawak, on the other hand, lived in western Venezuela and practiced an agricultural way of life based on cassava cultivation and fishing. They left significant cultural traces, including ceramics, art, and religious rites.

In the Andes of Venezuela lived the Timoto-Cuicas, an advanced culture that created terraced fields and developed a complex social and political system. They were known for their weaving skills and traded briskly with other indigenous peoples in the region.

The indigenous peoples of Venezuela each developed their own languages, religions and cultural practices. Their societies were often characterized by tribal structures in which chiefs or shamans played a central role. The relationship with nature and the spiritual connection to its environment were central to their way of life.

The arrival of Europeans in the 15th century led to dramatic changes for Venezuela's pre-Columbian cultures. Colonization brought diseases, wars and cultural assimilation that severely decimated indigenous populations and threatened their traditional ways of life. Nevertheless, many elements of pre-Columbian cultures have survived to this day and continue to shape Venezuela's cultural diversity.

The study and documentation of Venezuela's pre-Columbian cultures is an ongoing field of archaeological and anthropological research. New discoveries and insights are helping to preserve the rich heritage of these peoples and understand how they have shaped the history and development of today's Venezuela.

Arrival of the Europeans and colonial period

The arrival of Europeans in Venezuela in the 15th century marked a crucial turning point in the country's history. Christopher Columbus was one of the first Europeans to explore the coasts of Venezuela when he landed on the Paria Peninsula on his third voyage in 1498. The arrival of the Spaniards ushered in an era of colonization that would last over three centuries and leave deep scars on Venezuelan society, culture, and economy.

The Spaniards were in search of wealth and power and began to conquer and colonize the country. They established numerous settlements along the coast and inland to exploit the country's natural resources, including gold, silver, and precious stones. These colonial settlements served not only as military bases, but also as centers of missionary work and social control over the indigenous population.

Colonial rule was characterized by exploitation and oppression of the indigenous peoples, who were often forced to do forced labor on the plantations and in the mines. The encomienda was a system that allowed Spanish colonists to control and use indigenous labor, resulting in significant suffering and population losses among indigenous communities.

In 1527, Venezuela officially became part of the Spanish Viceroyalty of Peru and later became an independent captaincy under the administration of the Real Audiencia of Santo Domingo. Caracas became the administrative and economic center of the colony and experienced rapid expansion and development under Spanish rule.

During the colonial period, Venezuela became an important center of trade and culture in South America. The Spaniards brought with them not only their language, religion and systems of government, but also new plants, animals and technologies that permanently changed the lives of the indigenous and African population. This cultural mixing and interaction shaped Venezuela's identity and led to the emergence of a new Creole society.

Colonial rule finally ended in 1810, when Venezuela declared its independence from the Spanish crown. However, the colonial era left profound social, economic and cultural traces that continue to influence the country today. Researching and reflecting on this period is crucial to understanding Venezuela's complex history and its evolution into an independent nation.

Independence movements in the 19th century

The independence movements in the 19th century marked a significant turning point in Venezuela's history and were part of a broader movement in Latin America against Spanish colonial rule. The urge for independence had been intensified by social, economic and political grievances, which were exacerbated under Spanish rule.

The ideas of the Enlightenment and the examples of the American and French revolutions inspired Venezuelan patriots to rebel against colonial rule and demand an autonomous government. One of the leading figures of this movement was Francisco de Miranda, who is considered a pioneer of Venezuela's independence and made several unsuccessful attempts to lead a revolution against the Spanish.

However, the decisive moment came with the rise of Simón Bolívar, a charismatic leader and strategist who became known as "El Libertador". Bolívar successfully led a series of military campaigns against the Spanish troops and allied himself with other South American patriots such as José Antonio Páez and Antonio José de Sucre. Together they fought in battles such as the Battle of Carabobo (1821) and the Battle of Boyacá (1819), which were decisive for the course of the Wars of Independence.

Venezuelan independence was officially declared on July 5, 1811, although it could only be consolidated after several years of struggle and uncertainty. The loss and recapture of Caracas, as well as the strategic victories in the Andes and on the coast, were decisive for the course of events. Bolívar and his allies founded the Republic of Greater Colombia, which included Venezuela, Colombia, Ecuador, and Panama, and worked to develop a constitution and political system for the new nation.

However, Venezuela's independence was not an easy process and was accompanied by internal power struggles, political instability and economic challenges. Maintaining independence required both diplomatic skills and military determination to defend itself against the Spanish crown's ongoing attempts to reconquer the lost colonies.

The independence movements in the 19th century were not only a struggle against Spanish rule, but also a process of national identity formation and political consolidation of Venezuela. The ideals of freedom, equality and national sovereignty preached during this period continue to shape the memory of the historical significance of this era for modern Venezuela to this day.

The Road to the Republic: 20th Century to the Present

Venezuela's path to becoming a republic in the 20th century was marked by a number of political, economic and social challenges that still shape the country today. After independence from Spanish rule, a period of political instability and change began, marked by internal power struggles, military coups and economic turmoil.

The first half of the 20th century was marked by the dominance of political elites, who took turns in power and often introduced authoritarian forms of government. The oil industry, which had been booming since the beginning of the century, played an increasingly central role in Venezuela's economy, contributing to political and economic stability while increasing dependencies and inequalities.

In the 1940s, social and political unrest led to reform movements and the rise of popular leaders such as Rómulo Betancourt, who promoted democracy and took over a democratic government in 1958. This marked the beginning of an era of political stability and institutional development that became known as the Pacto de Punto Fijo, which included the political parties Conservatives, Social Democrats and Christian Democrats.

Oil revenues continued to flow into the treasury, enabling a period of economic prosperity and social programs that promoted education, health, and infrastructure. Venezuela became one of the wealthiest countries in Latin America, and Caracas developed into a modern metropolis with a growing middle class and a thriving cultural scene.

However, economic dependence on oil and increasing corruption became challenges in the 1980s, when falling oil prices led to an economic crisis. This triggered social unrest and political instability, which were exacerbated in the 1990s by repeated attempts at military takeovers and political scandals.

In the new millennium, Venezuela faced a profound political transformation under the leadership of Hugo Chávez. Chávez, a former military man and popular leader, championed socialist revolution and introduced sweeping reforms that reorganized the distribution of resources in favor of the poor and marginalized. However, his government was also controversial, dividing Venezuelan

21

society while exacerbating international tensions.

Venezuela's political landscape has remained turbulent to this day, with deep political polarization between supporters and opponents of Chavismo. Economic mismanagement, hyperinflation and supply crises have plunged the country into a severe crisis that has led to mass emigration and social tensions. Venezuela faces major challenges on the path to sustainable economic recovery and political stability, while the population continues to seek solutions for a better future.

Economic landscape and wealth of resources

Venezuela's economic landscape is strongly influenced by its extraordinary wealth of natural resources, especially oil. Venezuela has the largest oil reserves in the world, with an estimated deposit of over 300 billion barrels. These rich oil reserves have made the country one of the most important oil producers and exporters and play a central role in its economy.

The oil industry is the main engine of the Venezuelan economy and has had both positive and negative effects on the country. On the one hand, it has generated significant revenue that has been used to fund social programs, infrastructure projects, and educational initiatives. On the other hand, the heavy reliance on oil has made the economy vulnerable to fluctuations in global oil prices, which has created serious economic challenges in times of falling prices.

In addition to oil, Venezuela has a variety of other natural resources, including natural gas, iron, bauxite, gold, and diamonds. These commodities offer potential for diversification of the economy, but have often remained constrained by a lack of infrastructure and technological development.

23

Agriculture also plays an important role in the Venezuelan economy, although its share of gross domestic product is small compared to the oil industry. Venezuela produces a variety of agricultural products such as coffee, cocoa, sugar cane, rice and corn, with coffee cultivation historically playing a significant role.

However, Venezuela's economic landscape is not only shaped by its natural resources. Political instability, corruption and inefficient administration have led to challenges in economic governance and hampered the country's long-term development. In particular, social and economic inequalities are widespread and have contributed to the exacerbation of social tensions and political crises that Venezuela has experienced in recent decades.

The future of Venezuela's economic landscape remains uncertain and depends heavily on political decisions, international economic relations and the country's ability to use and diversify its natural resources efficiently. Despite the challenges and crises, there is potential for sustainable economic recovery and development, especially through investments in infrastructure, education and technology.

Social and demographic structures

Venezuela's social and demographic structures reflect a complex and multi-layered society characterized by ethnic diversity, social inequalities, and demographic challenges. The population of Venezuela is made up of a mix of different ethnic groups, including European, indigenous, and African roots, which have merged together throughout the country's history.

Venezuela's demographic structure shows a relatively young population, with a significant portion under the age of 30. Population density varies widely by region, with coastal areas and urban centers such as Caracas being the most densely populated, while rural and remote areas are sparsely populated.

Social inequalities are a prominent feature of Venezuelan society. While Venezuela built a growing middle class and a strong public education sector in the first decades of the 20th century, economic inequalities, corruption and an inefficient distribution of resources have led to a deep gap between rich and poor. This has contributed to the emergence of informal settlements and marginalised communities in cities, where many people live in poverty and have limited access to education, health care and basic services.

Urbanization trends have increased in recent decades, with more and more people moving to cities in search of better economic opportunities and living conditions. This has led to challenges in urban infrastructure and housing, especially in the poorer neighborhoods where government support is often limited.

Venezuela's ethnic diversity is reflected in a wide range of cultures, ranging from music, art, literature to cuisine. Traditional festivals and religious practices of different ethnic groups contribute to the country's cultural identity and show the diverse influences that have shaped Venezuela.

In recent years, Venezuela has faced a severe economic crisis that has led to a massive emigration of people who have left the country in search of better living conditions. This has created a challenge for the country's social structures, as families have been separated and many communities have lost their economic base.

Venezuela's social and demographic structures are dynamic and continue to evolve amid the current political, economic, and social challenges that characterize the country. The future of Venezuela depends heavily on how these structures can be further strengthened and developed to build a more stable and equitable society that benefits all citizens.

Education system and health care

Venezuela's education system and health care system are central pillars of the country's social infrastructure, which have a decisive influence on the quality of life and future prospects of the population. The education system is formally divided into different levels, starting with primary education, which is mandatory for children aged 6 to 14. The system also includes secondary education, which is divided into two cycles: the Basic Cycle (Bachillerato) and the Diversified Cycle, which provides specialized education.

The quality of educational institutions varies greatly depending on the region and funding. While urban schools in larger cities such as Caracas and Valencia often have better resources and teachers, schools in rural and remote areas often suffer from a lack of financial support and qualified teachers. In the past, the government has introduced programs to promote school education to improve access to education and reduce illiteracy.

The healthcare system in Venezuela is facing major challenges, despite a once well-established public health system. Historically, Venezuela has made significant progress in fighting disease and improving life expectancy.

In recent years, however, economic problems, political instability and a lack of investment have led to significant bottlenecks and a decline in the quality of health care.

The public health system suffers from a shortage of medical care, medicines and basic health services. Many hospitals and health centres are struggling to meet the needs of the population, especially in the poorer neighbourhoods and rural areas. Privatisation in the health sector has led to a further gap between those who have access to high-quality medical care and those who cannot.

The government has introduced various initiatives to improve healthcare, including programs to combat epidemics and promote preventive healthcare. Nevertheless, the health situation remains one of the most pressing challenges for Venezuela, as the population faces an increasing burden of chronic diseases and inadequate medical care.

The future of the education system and health care in Venezuela depends heavily on political decisions, economic recovery and international support. The challenges are great, but there is potential for improvement and reform to ensure that all Venezuelans have access to quality education and healthcare, regardless of their social or economic status.

Art and Literature: Cultural Expressions

Venezuela's art and literature are rich in diversity and reflect the country's history, cultural influences, and social challenges. The Venezuelan art scene has a long tradition, ranging from pre-Columbian influences to modern and contemporary art. Indigenous cultures such as the Caribs and the Arawak left behind impressive works of art in the form of ceramics, sculptures and murals that reflect their spiritual and everyday worlds.

During the colonial period, the Spanish settlers brought European artistic traditions and styles to Venezuela, which found expression in churches, monasteries and public buildings. These elaborate works, often in Baroque and Neoclassical styles, combined religious themes with local motifs and materials.

In the 19th century, Venezuelan art began a period of nationalization and modernization, influenced by the Romantic movement and nationalist ideas. Artists such as Arturo Michelena became known for their depictions of historical events and national symbols, which contributed to the formation of identity and the promotion of patriotism.

In the 20th century, Venezuelan art experienced a heyday of avant-garde and experimental movements. Artists such as Jesús Rafael Soto and Carlos Cruz-Diez became internationally known for their work in the field of kinetic art and Op Art, which used movement, light, and color to create visual effects and sensory experiences.

Venezuelan literature also reflects the cultural diversity and social realities of the country. Writers such as Rómulo Gallegos, known for his novel "Doña Bárbara", have shaped the national literary landscape and gained international recognition. The novel, which is set in the rural plains of Venezuela, addresses the social and political conflicts of the time and remains a classic of Latin American literature.

Modern Venezuelan writers continue this tradition by grappling with current issues such as migration, political oppression, and social inequality. Authors such as Alberto Barrera Tyszka and Karina Sainz Borgo have attracted international attention with their works by processing the complex reality of Venezuela in literature and making it accessible.

Venezuela's art and literature are facing challenges in the face of the country's current political and economic crises. Artists and writers struggle with limited resources, censorship, and the pressure to remain creative in difficult conditions. Nevertheless, Venezuela's cultural production remains vibrant and diverse, and the country's art and literature continue to contribute to the national identity and cultural heritage, which is recognized and appreciated beyond its borders.

Music and dance traditions

Venezuela's music and dance traditions are diverse and reflect the country's cultural diversity and regional differences. A significant part of Venezuelan music is characterized by a mixture of indigenous, African, and European influences that have merged throughout the country's history.

The traditional music of Venezuela spans a variety of styles and genres that vary by region. In rural areas, the joropo and llanera music styles are particularly popular. The joropo, accompanied by harp, maracas and cuatro (a type of guitar), is an energetic dance style that is often heard at rural festivals and celebrations. The llanera music, typical of the plains (llanos), is characterized by melodic chants and fast guitar rhythms that reflect the life and traditions of the llanos.

In the coastal regions of Venezuela, rhythms such as the gaita and the tamborera are common. The gaita, a type of traditional music from Zulia, is often played during the Christmas season and festivals and is known for its lively rhythms and cheerful melodies. The tamborera, on the other hand, is an Afro-Venezuelan rhythm played with drums and percussion and is often heard in religious ceremonies and cultural festivals.

Classical music also has a significant presence in Venezuela, especially through El Sistema, a nationally known music program that provides access to musical education to children from socially disadvantaged communities. The program has gained international recognition for its achievements, including the Simón Bolívar Youth Orchestra, which tours worldwide and has produced renowned conductors and soloists.

Venezuela also has a rich treasure trove of popular music, from salsa to reggaeton, which are popular in the country's urban centers. Cities like Caracas are known for their vibrant music scene, where local bands and artists fuse different styles together to create a modern and unique Venezuelan identity.

Venezuela's dance traditions also reflect the country's cultural diversity. Traditional dances such as the Tamunangue, originally from the Andean regions, and the San Juan Bautista, which is danced during the carnival season, are examples of Venezuela's rich dance culture. These dances are often associated with religious and cultural festivals and serve as an expression of the identity and community bond of the country's various ethno-cultural groups.

Overall, Venezuela's music and dance tradition remains a vibrant and dynamic element of national identity, encompassing both historical roots and contemporary influences. Despite the challenges the country faces, the cultural production of music and dance remains an important expression of Venezuela's joie de vivre and cultural diversity.

Religions and spiritual practices

Venezuela's religious and spiritual practices reflect a variety of faiths and traditions shaped by the country's history and cultural diversity. The dominant religion in Venezuela is Christianity, especially the Roman Catholic Church, which was introduced by the Spanish settlers during the colonial period. The majority of the Venezuelan population professes the Catholic faith, and many religious holidays and ceremonies have a permanent place in the Venezuelan calendar, such as the celebrations in honor of the Virgin of Coromoto, the patron saint of Venezuela.

In addition to Catholicism, there is a growing number of Protestants and Evangelicals who have increased in recent decades. These religious groups have had a significant impact on Venezuela's social and political landscape by offering alternative spiritual perspectives and social programs, often focused on poverty alleviation and social justice.

In addition, Afro-Venezuelan heritage plays a significant role in Venezuela's religious practice, especially in the form of syncretic religions such as Santería and Candomblé. These spiritual traditions combine African belief systems with Catholic elements and indigenous beliefs, and are often associated with rituals and ceremonies that emphasize the connection between humans, nature, and spirit.

The indigenous communities of Venezuela also practice their traditional religions, which are closely linked to nature and the spiritual belief in the ancestors. These practices include harvest-time rituals, healing ceremonies, and spiritual festivals designed to promote balance between humans and the environment.

In the urban centers of Venezuela, there is also an increasing presence of new religious movements, spiritual practices and esoteric teachings that respond to the needs of a modern and pluralistic society. These movements offer alternative forms of spirituality and personal growth, often integrating elements from different religious traditions and Eastern philosophies.

Venezuela's religious and spiritual practices reflect not only its beliefs, but also the social, political, and economic realities of the country. They play an important role in promoting a sense of community, solidarity and cultural identity in a society facing challenges such as economic instability and social inequality. Despite the diversity of Venezuela's religious landscape, the search for spiritual fulfillment and meaning remains a central element in the lives of many people in the country.

Everyday life and lifestyle of Venezuelans

The everyday life and lifestyle of Venezuelans is characterized by a mixture of cultural traditions, social challenges and individual adaptation strategies in the midst of a changing social and economic landscape. Life in Venezuela often revolves around family and close social networks, which play an important role in supporting and overcoming daily challenges.

The everyday working life of Venezuelans varies greatly depending on the profession, region and social class. In urban areas such as Caracas and Maracaibo, there are a wide variety of job opportunities, from office jobs to craft jobs and informal economic activities. Many Venezuelans are employed in small and medium-sized enterprises or work in the service sector, which makes up a significant part of the country's economy.

Working conditions are often challenging, especially in terms of working hours, wage levels and job security. In recent years, economic problems and political instability have led to an increase in informal employment and a decline in formal jobs, which has affected the living conditions of many Venezuelans.

The daily lifestyle of Venezuelans includes a variety of activities that are shaped by cultural traditions and modern influences. Food plays a central role in everyday Venezuelan life, with a variety of dishes based on local ingredients and traditional recipes. Arepas, empanadas, and pabellón criollo are just a few examples of the popular dishes enjoyed throughout Venezuela.

Social life in Venezuela is often marked by celebrations, festivals, and religious holidays that provide opportunities to meet with family and friends and cultivate cultural traditions. Carnival, Christmas and the festivities in honour of local patron saints are particularly significant events in the Venezuelan calendar, celebrated with music, dancing and a festive atmosphere.

The housing situation varies greatly depending on income and geographical location. While wealthier families live in comfortable homes or apartments in safe neighborhoods, many people in poorer communities live in informal settlements or slums, where access to basic services such as water, electricity, and sanitation is often limited.

The challenges of everyday life in Venezuela have led many people to become creative and flexible to meet daily needs and adapt to changing realities. Despite the economic and social challenges, Venezuelan society remains strong and resilient, with deep roots in cultural values, family ties and a proud national consciousness that carries people through difficult times.

Language and cultural diversity

Venezuela's language and cultural diversity reflect the country's complex history and ethnic makeup. The official language is Spanish, which is spoken by practically all Venezuelans and serves as a means of communication and official expression. Spanish came to Venezuela with the Spanish conquistadors in the 16th century and developed over the centuries into a regional variant that goes hand in hand with its own dialects and regional differences.

In addition to Spanish, there are a variety of indigenous languages spoken by the various indigenous peoples of Venezuela. These languages are often found in remote rural areas and play an important role in preserving the cultural identity and traditions of indigenous communities. Examples of indigenous languages in Venezuela include Warao, Wayuu, Pemón, and Yanomami, to name a few.

The cultural diversity of Venezuela is manifested not only in the language, but also in the customs, festivals, culinary traditions and artistic expressions of the various ethnic groups and communities in the country. This diversity is the result of a long history of migration, cultural interaction and ethnic mixing that has made Venezuela a melting pot of different cultural influences.

Afro-Venezuelan culture has also made a significant contribution to Venezuela's cultural diversity, particularly through its music, dances, and religious practices that reflect African and Caribbean influences. Traditions such as Santería and Tamborera have evolved over time and are present in many communities in the country, where they serve as an expression of cultural identity and resistance to oppression and discrimination.

Venezuelan society strives to protect and promote its cultural diversity by supporting programs that promote indigenous languages and cultures, as well as the preservation of the cultural heritage of Afro-Venezuelan communities. Despite challenges such as social tensions and economic instability, Venezuela's cultural diversity remains a central component of national identity and a source of pride and cultural enrichment for society as a whole.

Gastronomy and culinary traditions

Venezuela's gastronomy and culinary traditions reflect the diversity of its landscapes and the historical influences of indigenous, European, and African cultures. Venezuelan cuisine is characterized by a wealth of flavors, spices, and ingredients typical of the different regions of the country.

A central element of Venezuelan cuisine is arepas, a type of corn flatbread, which is prepared in many varieties and is considered a staple food in the Venezuelan diet. They are served filled with cheese, meat, avocado or other ingredients and are popular as breakfast, lunch and dinner.

Another popular dish is Pabellón Criollo, which is often considered the national dish of Venezuela. It consists of rice, black beans, fried beef and plant-based side dishes such as fried bananas or avocado. This dish is an example of the fusion of indigenous, African and European influences in Venezuelan cuisine.

Fish and seafood play an important role in the cuisine of Venezuela's coastal regions. Ceviche, a dish of raw fish or seafood marinated in lime juice and seasoned with onions, coriander and chilli, is particularly popular in coastal towns and is known for its fresh taste and vibrant flavours.

Venezuelan desserts are also varied and rich. Dulce de lechosa is a dessert made from green papayas, cooked in sugar syrup until soft and sweet. Quesillo is a type of pudding made from condensed milk, eggs, and caramel that is often served as a dessert and is appreciated for its creamy consistency and sweet taste.

Venezuela's culinary tradition also reflects the country's seasons and agricultural products. Fresh fruits such as papaya, mango, guava and pineapple are abundant throughout the year and are often enjoyed in juice, desserts or as a snack.

In recent years, Venezuelan cuisine has also absorbed influences from other Latin American countries, especially the Caribbean and Colombia. This has led to an expansion of the gastronomic offer and created new taste experiences for the Venezuelan population.

Despite economic challenges and supply shortages, Venezuela's culinary tradition remains an important part of the national identity and a source of pride for the people of the country. A love of food and an appreciation for local ingredients and recipes are essential components of the Venezuelan lifestyle and contribute to the country's cultural diversity.

The unique flora and fauna of Venezuela

The unique flora and fauna of Venezuela represent an abundance of biodiversity, which is shaped by the diverse geographical and climatic conditions of the country. Venezuela stretches from the tropical rainforests of the Amazon basin in the south to the arid coastal regions of the Caribbean and the cooler Andes in the west of the country. This diversity of habitats supports a rich range of animal and plant species that are both endemic and unique to the region.

The Amazon basin, which makes up much of southern Venezuela, is home to some of the most biodiverse rainforests in the world. This region is home to thousands of plant species, including giant mahogany trees, lianas, orchids, and countless species of ferns and palm trees. The wildlife is equally impressive, with a variety of mammals such as jaguar, anteater, tapir and numerous species of monkeys, including the rare golden lion tamarin.

Mangrove forests stretch along the coastal regions of Venezuela, providing important habitats for a variety of waterfowl, fish and crustaceans. These areas play a crucial role in the ecosystem of the coastline and serve as spawning grounds for fish as well as protection against coastal erosion.

The Andean region in western Venezuela is known for its alpine habitats and diverse flora, ranging from lush cloud forests at lower altitudes to alpine grasslands and high mountain forests. Specialized plant species such as Puya raimondii, a huge species of bromeliads, thrive here, as well as various species of orchids and tree ferns.

Venezuela is also home to a rich bird life with over 1,300 species of birds, including the harpy, an imposing bird of prey and one of the largest birds of prey in the world. The country's tropical forests and coastlines provide shelter and food sources for numerous migratory birds and endemic species.

The importance of nature conservation and the sustainable use of natural resources has become increasingly important in Venezuela in light of the challenges posed by deforestation, mining and illegal poaching. Government programs and conservation organizations work together to protect important ecosystems and preserve the country's biodiversity for generations to come.

Overall, Venezuela's unique flora and fauna remains a source of pride and fascination, which not only arouses scientific interest, but also plays an important role in the country's ecological balance and cultural identity. Venezuela's diversity of habitats and species is a treasure that must be protected and nurtured in order to preserve the country's natural beauty and ecological integrity.

Nature reserves and ecotourism

Nature reserves and ecotourism are playing an increasingly important role in Venezuela, a country with rich biodiversity and scenic beauty. These areas are critical to protecting endangered species, preserving natural habitats, and promoting sustainable development practices in a rapidly changing world.

One of Venezuela's best-known nature reserves is the Canaima National Park in the southeast of the country, which is a UNESCO World Heritage Site. The park covers an area of over 30,000 square kilometers and is home to the famous Angel Falls, the highest waterfall in the world. Canaima is known for its spectacular mesas, known as tepuis, as well as its diverse flora and fauna, including rare species of orchids and endemic animals such as the Canaima frog.

Another important nature reserve is the Morrocoy National Park on the coast of Venezuela, known for its Caribbean beaches, coral reefs and mangrove forests. The park provides habitat for a variety of marine animals such as dolphins, manatees, and a variety of fish and coral species. The protection of these marine ecosystems is crucial for the conservation of biodiversity and the sustainable use of coastal resources.

Ecotourism has gained traction in Venezuela, offering visitors the opportunity to experience the country's natural beauty while helping to protect the environment. Tourists can stay in lodges and eco-camps that operate according to ecological standards and are often managed by local communities. These facilities offer guided hikes, bird watching, boat trips, and other sustainable activities that connect visitors with nature and contribute to the local economy.

The government of Venezuela has implemented programs to promote conservation and develop ecotourism to protect the environment while creating economic opportunities for local communities. These initiatives aim to raise awareness of the importance of environmental protection and promote the conservation of the country's natural resources.

In addition to the large nature reserves, there are numerous smaller protected areas and reserves throughout Venezuela that protect a variety of ecosystems, from tropical rainforests and deserts to wetlands and alpine regions. These areas play an essential role in the conservation of biodiversity and provide important habitats for endangered species such as the jaguar, the giant otter and the giant condor.

Overall, nature conservation and ecotourism in Venezuela are not only of ecological importance, but also of economic and social importance. By protecting and sustainably using the country's natural resources, long-term environmental and economic benefits can be created for Venezuelan society, while preserving the beauty and uniqueness of the natural environment.

The capital Caracas: past and present

The capital of Venezuela, Caracas, is not only the political and economic center of the country, but also a cultural and historical centerpiece that spans a turbulent past and a multi-layered present. Founded in 1567 by the Spanish conquistador Diego de Losada, Caracas has a rich colonial history behind it, marked by its strategic location in a fertile valley at the foot of the Avila Mountains.

Over the course of the colonial period, Caracas developed into a major trading center for gold and cocoa, attracting settlers from different parts of Spain who contributed to the cultural diversity of the city. During this period, magnificent colonial buildings were erected, some of which have survived to this day, including the Cathedral of Caracas and the historic center of the city.

In the 19th century, Caracas played a key role in South America's independence movements against Spanish rule. Simón Bolívar, the great independence leader, was born in Caracas and played a crucial role in the liberation of Venezuela and other South American countries from Spanish colonial rule. His influence can be felt throughout the city, from monuments and street names to museums dedicated to his legacy.

In the 20th century, Caracas experienced rapid growth and became a modern metropolis with a growing population and an expanding economy. The oil industry played a crucial role in the economic development of the city and the country as a whole, leading to a construction boom and urban expansion. Skyscrapers and modern architecture now characterize the cityscape of Caracas, which is considered one of the most populous cities in Latin America.

However, despite its growth and development, Caracas faces challenges such as social inequality, economic instability, and an increasing crime rate. These problems have affected urban life and led to tensions within the population as the government and local authorities strive to find solutions to these challenges.

Culturally, Caracas is a dynamic center for art, music, and literature, home to a vibrant cultural scene characterized by renowned museums, galleries, and theaters. The Venezuelan capital has produced numerous important figures, including artists, writers and musicians, who have gained national and international recognition and contributed to the country's cultural identity.

Today, Caracas remains a place of change and challenges, but also of opportunities and cultural riches. The history and present of this vibrant metropolis reflect the diversity and complexity of Venezuela and are a central part of the country's national identity and collective memory.

Maracaibo: commercial center and cultural heart

Maracaibo, Venezuela's second-largest city, is not only an important commercial center, but also a cultural heart of the country. Founded in 1529 by German colonists led by Ambrosius Ehinger, the city quickly became an important hub for trade between Europe and the New World. The location on Lake Maracaibo, the largest inland lake in South America, offered strategic advantages for trade and contributed to the economic development of the region.

The city became known for its wealth of natural resources, especially the oil fields in the area, which made Maracaibo a key player in the Venezuelan oil industry. Oil exports have shaped the economy of the city and the entire country, leading to rapid growth, which has been further supported by modern infrastructures such as the Maracaibo Bridge, one of the longest bridges in Latin America.

Culturally, Maracaibo is known for its vibrant music scene, which includes traditional styles such as gaita zuliana, a local music genre that is particularly popular during the Christmas season. The city is also home to important cultural institutions such as the Museo de Arte

Contemporáneo del Zulia and the Teatro Baralt, which promote a wide variety of artistic expressions and contribute to the cultural diversity of the region.

Architecturally, Maracaibo is characterized by a mixture of colonial buildings in the historic center and modern high-rise buildings along the waterfront. The Maracaibo Cathedral and other historic buildings are testimonies to the city's rich history and cultural heritage, while new developments such as the Sambil Shopping Center and the Centro Ciudad Comercial Tamanaco reflect the economic dynamism of the region.

The city is also known for its culinary specialties, including seafood dishes from Lake Maracaibo and local delicacies such as patacones, deep-fried plantains that are often served as a side dish. This gastronomic diversity reflects the cultural fusion that makes Maracaibo a symbol of Venezuela's diversity.

Despite its economic importance and cultural riches, Maracaibo faces challenges such as infrastructure modernization, social inequalities, and environmental issues, including Lake Maracaibo's threat of pollution and dwindling water resources.

However, the government and local organizations are working to address these challenges and secure the future of the city as an important commercial and cultural center.

Overall, Maracaibo remains a dynamic and multifaceted city that embodies both historical heritage and modern progress. Its role as a commercial center and cultural heart is further strengthened by its unique location, economic importance and cultural diversity, which make it an indispensable part of the Venezuelan landscape.

Valencia and industrial development

Valencia, one of the most important cities in Venezuela, has become a center of industrial development and economic activity over the years. Conveniently located in the central part of the country, about 150 kilometers west of Caracas, the city played a crucial role in the development of the Venezuelan economy, especially in the field of manufacturing.

The origins of Valencia date back to colonial times, when the city served as an important trading point for agricultural products and a crossroads for trade routes. With the arrival of the railway in the late 19th century, Valencia experienced a boom as transport options were improved for the export of coffee, cocoa and sugar cane, which were grown in the surrounding fertile region.

In the 20th century, Valencia became a focal point for industrial production, especially after Venezuela's rise as a major oil exporter. The proximity to the country's oil fields favored the settlement of industries such as petrochemicals, metallurgy, food processing and automotive production. The city is home to large industrial complexes and factories that contribute to the country's heavy industry and provide jobs for a significant number of workers.

Of particular note is Valencia's automotive industry, which plays a significant role in the city's economy. Various car manufacturers have set up production facilities in Valencia, including General Motors, which produce vehicles there for the local market and for export. This has promoted the economic stability of the city and made Valencia an important center for the automotive industry in Latin America.

Culturally, Valencia offers a mix of traditional and modern architecture, as well as a vibrant arts scene promoted by museums, galleries and cultural events. The city prides itself on its cultural events such as the annual Gran Feria de Valencia, a festival that celebrates music, dance, crafts and local cuisine, attracting visitors from all over the region.

However, in recent years, Valencia has faced challenges such as traffic problems, environmental pollution and economic instability. The government and local organizations are working to address these challenges and improve the quality of life in the city, while strengthening the industrial base and economic dynamism.

Overall, Valencia remains a symbol of Venezuela's industrial strength and a vibrant center of economic activity and cultural diversity. Its role in the country's history and development is undeniable, and its future depends on its ability to address the challenges of the 21st century and continue to be a driving force for growth and progress.

Mérida: The gateway to the Andes

Mérida, the capital of the state of Mérida in Venezuela, is known as the gateway to the Andes and is considered one of the oldest cities in Venezuela with a rich history and cultural heritage. Founded in 1558 by Juan Rodríguez Suárez, the city is known for its spectacular location in the Venezuelan Andes, which makes it a popular destination for tourists and adventurers from all over the world.

The geographical location of Mérida is noteworthy, as it is located at an altitude of about 1,600 meters above sea level and is surrounded by majestic mountains, including Pico Bolívar, the highest mountain in Venezuela. This unique geographical location has made Mérida a hub for mountain sports such as hiking, climbing, mountaineering and paragliding, with the nearby Sierra Nevada National Park offering a variety of hiking trails and nature trails that attract adventurers and nature lovers alike.

The city is also known for its colonial architecture, which is well preserved in the historic buildings in the center of Mérida. The Cathedral of Mérida, built in the 18th century, as well as the historic center with its cobbled streets and old squares, bear witness to the Spanish colonial era and give the city a charming and authentic character.

Mérida is also a major educational center in Venezuela, which is home to the Universidad de Los Andes (ULA), one of the most prestigious universities in the country. Known for its research and teaching in science, technology, humanities, and the arts, ULA attracts students from across the country who seek a high-quality academic education.

Culturally, Mérida offers a rich variety of traditions and artistic expressions, including music, dance, theatre and crafts. The city is known for its annual festivals and celebrations, including the Feria Internacional del Sol, a festival that celebrates the culture of the Andean region and attracts visitors from all over the world.

From a tourist point of view, Mérida is a popular destination for adventurers and nature lovers who want to explore the spectacular scenery of the Andes. The city offers a variety of accommodation, from cozy guesthouses to luxurious hotels, to suit the needs and budgets of visitors.

In recent years, Mérida has struggled with challenges such as infrastructure deficiencies and economic instability, which have impacted urban life and quality of life. Still, Mérida remains a symbol of Venezuela's natural beauty and a cultural oasis in the Andes that offers a unique blend of history, nature, and hospitality.

The historical significance of Ciudad Bolívar

Ciudad Bolívar, formerly known as Angostura, is a city of outstanding historical importance in Venezuela. Founded in 1764, it played a key role in the country's history, especially during the independence movements of the 19th century. The city was named in honor of Simón Bolívar, the national hero of Venezuela and liberator of many South American countries from Spanish colonial rule.

Ciudad Bolívar's strategic location on the banks of the Orinoco River contributed significantly to its historical importance, as it functioned as an important trade and transport hub. The river provided access to areas deep in the Venezuelan jungle and played a crucial role in the exchange of goods between the interior and coastal regions.

During the colonial period, Ciudad Bolívar was an important center for the gold and diamond trade, making it an economic engine in the region. The city grew rapidly and became a cultural center that promoted art, architecture, and music, which is reflected in the well-preserved historic buildings in the center of the city.

In the 19th century, Ciudad Bolívar became the political center of Venezuela when the Congress of Angostura was held there in 1817. At this historic congress, Simón Bolívar presented his famous speech in which he formulated his vision for independence and the unification of South America. This speech marked a turning point in the history of the continent and paved the way for independence movements throughout South America.

The city was also the scene of important battles during the Venezuelan Wars of Independence, including the Battle of San Félix in 1817 and the Battle of Ciudad Bolívar in 1819, which contributed decisively to the victory of the patriotic forces led by Simón Bolívar over the Spanish troops.

Today, Ciudad Bolívar is a living monument to Venezuela's history, attracting visitors with its well-preserved colonial architecture, museums, and memorials that commemorate the heroic deeds and visions of the independence fighters. The city remains an important cultural and historical center in the heart of Venezuela, offering a unique insight into the country's past and development.

Barquisimeto Capital of Culture

Barquisimeto, also known as "the music city" of Venezuela, is considered one of the country's most important cultural metropolises. It is located in the western part of Venezuela and is the capital of the state of Lara. Founded in 1552, the city has a rich history and a diverse cultural scene that has made it a magnet for art, music, and theater.

Culturally, Barquisimeto is known for its vibrant musical tradition, especially the Festival Internacional de Música de Barquisimeto, which attracts musicians from all over the world every year. The city has produced important musicians and composers and is famous for its contribution to Venezuelan musical culture, especially in the field of traditional Venezuelan music such as Joropo and Gaita.

Architecturally, Barquisimeto is a mix of modern buildings and well-preserved colonial structures that reflect its rich history. Attractions include the Cathedral of Barquisimeto, an impressive example of colonial architecture, as well as the Obelisk of Barquisimeto, a city landmark built in honor of the city's founding.

The city is also proud of its cultural institutions such as the Museo de Barquisimeto, which houses an extensive collection of artworks and artifacts from the region, as well as the Teatro Juares, a renowned theater that hosts a variety of cultural events and performances.

Barquisimeto is also known for its culinary diversity, ranging from traditional Venezuelan dishes such as arepas and hallacas to international cuisines. The local cuisine reflects the diversity of cultures that have shaped the city, from indigenous influences to European colonial times and modern trends.

Economically, Barquisimeto is an important industrial location in Venezuela, especially in the field of food processing, textile industry and trade. The city has one of the largest markets in the country, the Mercado Mayorista de Barquisimeto, which plays a significant role in the trade of agricultural products and other goods.

However, Barquisimeto also faces challenges such as economic instability and social inequalities that affect the quality of life of its residents. The government and local organizations are working to address these challenges and secure the future of the city as a cultural and economic center.

Overall, Barquisimeto remains a symbol of Venezuela's cultural diversity and artistic creativity. Its role as the country's cultural capital is strengthened by its rich history, diverse music scene, and vibrant cultural landscape, which makes it an indispensable part of Venezuelan culture and identity.

The coastal town of Puerto La Cruz and its beaches

Puerto La Cruz, a coastal city in northeastern Venezuela, is famous for its beautiful beaches and its location on the Caribbean Sea. The city was founded in the 17th century and has since become a popular tourist destination, attracting visitors from all over the world who want to enjoy the sun, sand, and crystal clear waters.

The beaches of Puerto La Cruz offer a variety of recreational options for visitors. Among the most famous beaches is Playa El Faro, which is known for its calm waters and picturesque scenery. Here, visitors can relax, swim, and practice water sports such as jet skiing and scuba diving.

Another popular beach is Playa Lido, which is known for its livelier atmosphere and is often visited by locals and tourists alike. This beach regularly hosts cultural events and concerts that attract visitors.

In addition to the beaches, Puerto La Cruz also offers a variety of leisure activities and attractions. Parque Nacional Mochima is close to the city and is known for its unspoiled nature and rich marine wildlife. Here, visitors can take boat trips to explore the surrounding islands and reefs or simply enjoy the spectacular scenery.

The town itself has a lively atmosphere with a variety of restaurants, bars and shops offering local specialties and handicrafts. The port of Puerto La Cruz is also an important transshipment point for the export of oil and other goods, which contributes to the economic dynamism of the city.

Culturally, Puerto La Cruz is characterized by a mixture of Spanish and Caribbean culture, which is reflected in the city's architecture, music and festivals. Various events take place throughout the year, including the Festival Internacional de Música, which attracts artists from all over the world, as well as traditional festivals and carnival celebrations.

Despite its appeal as a tourist destination, Puerto La Cruz faces challenges such as pollution and social inequalities that affect the quality of life of its residents. However, the government and local organizations are working to address these issues and promote the sustainable development of the city in order to maintain its status as one of the most beautiful coastal cities in Venezuela.

The islands of Los Roques

The island world of Los Roques, a Venezuelan national park, covers an area of about 221,120 hectares and includes more than 300 islands, islets and sandbanks in the Caribbean Sea. This archipelago is known for its unspoiled beauty, turquoise waters and fine sandy beaches that make it a paradise for nature lovers and sun worshippers.

The history of Los Roques goes back a long way and is closely linked to Venezuela's maritime history. During the colonial period, the island chain served as a refuge for pirates and later as a strategic anchorage for merchant ships. Today, it is a protected area that attracts visitors from all over the world who want to experience the unspoiled nature and biodiversity of the region.

The islands of Los Roques offer a variety of activities for visitors, including snorkeling, diving, sport fishing, and sailing. The waters around the islands are known for their clear visibility and rich marine life with coral reefs, tropical fish, rays and sea turtles. Diving lovers can enjoy the numerous diving spots that are suitable for both beginners and experienced divers.

The largest island of the group is Gran Roque, which is also the administrative center of the national park. Here, visitors will find a selection of accommodation, restaurants and shops to cover all needs. Gran Roque is also the starting point for boat trips to the surrounding islands, where visitors can explore secluded beaches and coves.

The flora and fauna of Los Roques are unique and include a wide variety of plant species adapted to the salty environment and tropical climate. Many of the islands are also breeding grounds for sea turtles and home to a variety of seabirds, including pelicans, frigate birds, and cormorants.

Tourism plays a significant role in Los Roques' economy, with visitors from all over the world helping to strengthen the local economy. At the same time, the national park faces challenges such as pollution and overfishing, which can threaten the fragile ecosystems of the islands. However, the government and local organizations are committed to the protection and sustainable development of Los Roques in order to preserve its natural beauty and biodiversity for future generations.

The Orinoco: the lifeline of the country

The Orinoco, one of the longest rivers in South America, is the lifeline of Venezuela and an essential source of water, transport and biodiversity. With a length of about 2,250 kilometers, it flows through the heart of the country and plays a crucial role in the ecological and economic systems of the region.

Originally revered by indigenous peoples as the "goddess of water", the Orinoco River has a rich cultural significance for Venezuelan society. It rises in the state of Amazonas near the Brazilian border and flows through the Venezuelan plains before flowing into the Atlantic Ocean in a huge delta.

The Orinoco River basin covers about 880,000 square kilometers, which accounts for about 30% of Venezuela's land area. This vast area encompasses a variety of habitats, from tropical rainforests to savannahs and swamps, which support remarkable biodiversity. The river and its tributaries are home to a variety of species, including river dolphins, caimans, giant otters, and a variety of fish and waterfowl.

Economically, the Orinoco plays a key role in the transport of goods and raw materials. River navigation is an important part of Venezuela's infrastructure, providing access to remote areas that are difficult to reach by land. Traditional communities along the river use it for fishing, agriculture and transport, being closely linked to the natural rhythms and tides of the river.

The Orinoco is also a significant source of energy, especially through the hydroelectric power plants that have been built along the river to generate electricity. This energy supply plays a central role in the Venezuelan economy and contributes to the country's industrial development.

However, environmental threats such as deforestation, mining and oil extraction pose a serious threat to the health of the Orinoco and its ecosystems. The government and environmental organizations are committed to the protection and sustainable use of the river in order to preserve its vitality and importance as a natural resource.

Overall, the Orinoco remains not only an economic backbone of Venezuela, but also a cultural and ecological symbol that has shaped history and life in the country for thousands of years. Its future depends on the responsible use and protection of its unique natural resources to preserve them for future generations.

The Andean region of Venezuela

The Andean region of Venezuela, a majestic mountain system, stretches across the western part of the country and plays a central role in its geographical, cultural, and environmental diversity. This mountain range forms part of the longest mountain range in the world and spans several countries in South America, creating a variety of unique landscapes and habitats in Venezuela.

The Andes are geologically young and were formed millions of years ago by the collision of the South American and Caribbean plates. They stretch over a length of about 2,800 kilometers through Venezuela, Colombia, Ecuador, Peru, Bolivia, and Chile and reach heights of more than 5,000 meters above sea level. In Venezuela, the Andes form a dramatic backdrop that stretches from the flat plains of the Maracaibo Basin to the peaks of the highest mountains.

The highest peaks in Venezuela can be found in the Andes, including Pico Bolívar with an altitude of 4,978 meters, Pico Humboldt with 4,942 meters and Pico Bonpland with 4,883 meters. These peaks are not only challenges for mountaineers, but also important sources of water and biodiversity in the region. The Andean region of Venezuela is home to a variety of ecosystems, ranging from humid cloud forests at higher elevations to arid deserts at lower elevations. This diversity of habitats supports a rich biodiversity, including rare orchids, hummingbirds, condors, cougars, and tapirs. The people who live in the Venezuelan Andes often belong to indigenous peoples such as the Pemon, Yanomami, and Timoto-Cuicas. These communities have preserved their traditional ways of life and cultural practices, which are heavily influenced by the natural environment and the seasons. Agriculture, livestock and handicrafts are traditional livelihoods in this region, which is often characterized by isolated settlements and small towns.

In terms of tourism, the Andean region of Venezuela is a popular destination for adventure and nature tourism. Visitors can enjoy hiking, mountaineering, bird watching, and visiting historic cities such as Mérida, which is known for its cable car that offers spectacular views of the surrounding mountains.

The Andes are not only a geographical feature of Venezuela, but also a cultural heritage and an important resource for the country's sustainable development. The government and local organizations are committed to protecting this fragile environment to preserve its beauty and ecological importance for future generations.

The Amazon rainforest and its inhabitants

The Amazon rainforest, which covers a considerable part of Venezuela, is one of the most biodiverse and ecologically important regions on earth. This vast ecosystem spans millions of square kilometers in South America, with the Venezuelan part being home to a variety of unique habitats and animal species.

The Amazon rainforests are known for their immense biodiversity, which includes a treasure trove of plants, animals, and microorganisms, many of which have not even been classified yet. This region is home to more than 40,000 species of plants, 1,300 species of birds, 3,000 species of fish and an unknown number of insect species. Large mammals such as jaguars, tapirs, anteaters, and howler monkeys roam the dense forests, while rivers such as the Orinoco and Amazon rivers support the lives of countless species of fish and amphibians.

The people who live in the Venezuelan Amazon are often indigenous communities that have been closely connected to nature for centuries. These peoples, including the Yanomami, Piaroa, and Ye'kuana, have developed traditional ways of life and knowledge of herbal medicine that help them survive in this challenging environment. Hunting, fishing, fruit collection and agriculture are traditional livelihoods that are closely linked to the natural rhythms of the rainforest.

The Amazon rainforest plays a crucial role in the global climate system, as it acts as a carbon sink and makes a significant contribution to regulating the Earth's climate. The vegetation of the rainforest stores carbon dioxide and produces oxygen, which is crucial for the balance of the atmosphere.

Despite its ecological importance, the Venezuelan Amazon rainforest faces various threats, including deforestation, mining, illegal land use, and the construction of roads and dams. These activities lead to a loss of biodiversity, deterioration of water quality and a threat to the livelihoods of indigenous communities.

Government agencies and environmental organizations are working together to strengthen the protection of the Amazon rainforest and promote sustainable development practices that preserve both the natural environment and the livelihoods of local populations. Preserving this unique ecosystem is crucial, not only for the future of Venezuela, but for the health of the entire planet.

The Caribbean coast and its attractions

The Caribbean coast of Venezuela stretches along a scenic stretch of several hundred kilometers and offers a wealth of natural and cultural attractions. This coastal region not only attracts tourists, but is also a major economic center of the country, benefiting from fishing, tourism, and the oil industry.

The beaches of the Caribbean coast are famous for their turquoise waters and fine sandy beaches, which offer ideal conditions to relax and unwind. Popular coastal resorts such as the islands of Los Roques and the Paraguaná Peninsula are known for their pristine beaches and rich maritime diversity. The coastal waters are also a haven for water sports such as diving, snorkeling, sailing and sport fishing.

Apart from the beaches, the Caribbean coast of Venezuela offers a variety of historical and cultural attractions. Cities such as Caracas and La Guaira are significant historic centers that offer rich colonial architecture and museums with artworks and artifacts from the country's history. Caracas' Old Town, known as Casco Histórico, is a UNESCO World

Heritage Site and is home to historic buildings dating back to the Spanish colonial era.

The coastal areas are also culturally diverse, marked by the traditional way of life of the coastal inhabitants and their close connection to the sea. Fishing villages such as Chichiriviche and Puerto Colombia are well-known centers for Venezuelan coastal culture, where visitors can enjoy local dishes based on fresh seafood.

In addition to its natural beauty and cultural appeal, the Caribbean coast also plays a crucial role in Venezuela's trade and transportation. The port of La Guaira is one of the most important commercial ports in the country and serves as a gateway to international markets. The oil industry also uses the coastal region to transport and ship crude oil, which is a significant source of income for the Venezuelan economy.

However, the future of Venezuela's Caribbean coast faces challenges, including pollution, overfishing, and climate change that threaten natural resources and the livelihoods of coastal residents. The government and environmental organizations are committed to promoting sustainable development practices and preserving the unique beauty and diversity of this region.

Overall, Venezuela's Caribbean coast remains one of the country's most fascinating and diverse regions, valued for both its natural treasures and cultural significance. It offers visitors and locals alike a rich experience that reflects the history, nature, and way of life of the people along this unique coastline.

Angel Falls: The highest waterfall in the world

Angel Falls, or Salto Ángel, is undoubtedly one of the most spectacular natural wonders of Venezuela and the world. With a height of around 979 meters and a free fall of about 807 meters, Angel Falls is the highest waterfall on earth. It is located in the Canaima National Park in the southern part of Venezuela and is part of the UNESCO World Heritage Site.

The origin of the name Angel Falls goes back to Jimmy Angel, an American pilot who discovered the waterfall in 1933 during a flying expedition over the region. Since then, Salto Ángel has gained international fame and attracts thousands of tourists annually who are fascinated by the majestic beauty and unspoiled surroundings.

The waterfall plunges from a tepui, a prominent table mountain of the region, forming a spectacular curtain of sparkling water that falls into the jungle below. This phenomenon makes Angel Falls not only an impressive sight, but also a significant hydrological and ecological source for the surrounding region.

Canaima National Park, where Angel Falls is located, is also home to rich biodiversity, including rare plant species, exotic animals, and a variety of bird species. The landscape around the waterfall is characterized by lush rainforest and savannah-like plains that contrast with the steep rock walls and cascading water.

Access to Angel Falls is often only possible via airplanes or boat tours, as the remote location and difficult accessibility of Canaima National Park pose a challenge for visitors. Still, the trip to this natural wonder is an unforgettable experience that attracts adventure seekers from all over the world.

The local indigenous people, especially the Pemon, consider Angel Falls to be a sacred place and part of their cultural identity. Their traditions and stories reflect the close connection to the natural elements and the spiritual significance of the waterfall.

The protection of Angel Falls and its surrounding ecosystem is crucial to the preservation of this unique natural heritage. The Venezuelan government and environmental organizations are working together to promote sustainable practices and minimize the threats posed by human intervention, such as mining and deforestation.

Overall, Angel Falls remains not only an impressive geographical feature of Venezuela, but also a symbol of the beauty and fragility of the natural world. Its presence in the Canaima National Park attracts visitors who want to experience the power and majesty of nature in its purest form.

National parks and protected areas

Venezuela's national parks and protected areas are an important source of conservation for the country's biodiversity and natural resources. They encompass a variety of ecosystems ranging from the mountains of the Andes to the deserts of the coastal regions to the rainforests of the Amazon. These protected areas play a crucial role in the preservation of Venezuela's unique animal and plant species and contribute to maintaining ecological balance.

One of Venezuela's most prominent national parks is Canaima National Park, known for Angel Falls, the highest waterfall in the world. Covering an area of over 30,000 square kilometers, Canaima is home to a variety of landforms, including mesas, rivers, waterfalls, and tropical forests. This park is also home to many indigenous communities, including the Pemon, who maintain a close relationship with the natural environment and preserve traditional ways of life.

Another important national park is the Henri Pittier National Park, which is the oldest national park in Venezuela and stretches along the coastal cordillera. Henri Pittier protects a variety of ecosystems, including tropical rainforests, coastal mangroves, and cloud forests. It is known for its biodiversity, including a large number of endemic plant and animal species that are unique to this region.

In the south of Venezuela is the Sierra Nevada National Park, which is known for its glacial lakes and the diversity of alpine vegetation. This park protects Venezuela's highest peaks, including Pico Bolívar and Pico Humboldt, and is a popular destination for mountaineers and nature lovers.

Venezuela's coastal areas are also protected by protected areas that contribute to the conservation of marine habitats and biodiversity. The Los Roques archipelago, a national park and marine reserve, is known for its coral reefs, its beaches and its diverse marine fauna. This park is a popular destination for divers and snorkelers who want to explore the underwater world of the Caribbean.

The Venezuelan government and various non-governmental organizations are actively working to protect and expand the country's protected areas in order to conserve natural resources and combat the threats posed by illegal land use, mining and poaching. Despite these efforts, Venezuela's national parks and protected areas face challenges such as funding conservation measures, managing and monitoring the areas, and managing social and economic impacts on local populations.

Overall, Venezuela's national parks and protected areas play a crucial role in preserving the country's biodiversity and natural ecosystems. They not only provide important habitats for plants and animals, but also recreational opportunities for visitors and help promote sustainable tourism that protects natural resources while supporting local communities.

Architectural jewels and historical buildings

Venezuela is home to a variety of architectural gems and historical structures that bear witness to its rich cultural and colonial history. One of the most outstanding examples is undoubtedly the old town of Caracas, known as Casco Histórico. Here you will find colonial buildings from the 16th century, which are influenced by Spanish architecture and represent a fascinating mix of European influence and local traditions.

A striking example is the Cathedral of Caracas, one of the oldest cathedrals in South America, whose construction began in 1666. The cathedral displays Baroque and neoclassical elements and houses valuable religious artifacts and works of art.

Another architectural gem is the building of the Universidad Central de Venezuela in Caracas, designed by the famous architect Carlos Raúl Villanueva. This university is an outstanding example of 20th-century modern architecture and has been declared a UNESCO World Heritage Site due to its architectural and urban planning qualities.

The city of Coro, one of Venezuela's oldest cities and also a UNESCO World Heritage Site, is home to well-preserved examples of colonial architecture. Here, the narrow streets, colorful houses and historic squares are a reflection of the Spanish colonial era and its architectural tradition.

The historic city of Ciudad Bolívar, on the banks of the Orinoco River, is also home to notable architectural treasures, including the Cathedral and Casa San Isidro, an 18th-century historic house that serves as a museum and offers insight into the life and architecture of the time.

Venezuelan architecture reflects not only European influences, but also adaptation to local climatic conditions and cultural traditions. This is particularly evident in the traditional haciendas, agricultural estates with spacious courtyards and shady verandas, which often serve as a sign of prosperity and the local way of life.

Modern architecture has also gained a foothold in Venezuela, especially in major cities such as Caracas, Maracaibo, and Valencia, where skyscrapers, shopping malls, and modern residential complexes dominate the cityscape. These structures reflect the country's dynamic development and its ambitions in the field of urban planning and architecture.

Despite the diversity and richness of Venezuelan architecture, many historic buildings and monuments face challenges such as neglect, urbanization, and environmental pressures. Efforts to preserve and restore these architectural treasures are essential to preserve Venezuela's cultural heritage and make it accessible to future generations.

Carnival and traditional festivals

Carnival and traditional festivals play a central role in Venezuela's cultural life and reflect the diversity of regional customs and traditions. Carnival, especially in the big cities like Caracas, Maracaibo and La Guaira, is a time of exuberant celebrations and colorful parades. The festivities officially begin on Ash Wednesday and continue until the Tuesday before Lent, with peaks reaching in the last week before Lent.

In Caracas, the carnival is characterized by street parades, music, dance and elaborate costumes. The participants, often organized in groups and known as "comparsas", perform choreographies that integrate local music and traditional dances such as the "Danza de los Diablos". These dances often have religious or historical roots and tell stories through movement and music.

A unique feature of the Venezuelan Carnival is the "Burriquita" in Carúpano, in the state of Sucre, where participants are dressed as horses and accompany a parade inspired by religious traditions. These performances mix African, indigenous and Spanish elements and are a living example of Venezuela's cultural diversity.

In addition to Carnival, there are numerous traditional festivals that are celebrated regionally and reflect local customs and rituals. In Mérida, for example, the festival of the Virgen de la Candelaria is celebrated, which is associated with processions, music and traditional dances. The event attracts pilgrims from all over the region and is an important event in the religious calendar.

In the state of Zulia, the festival in honor of the Virgen de Chiquinquirá is particularly significant, combined with boat trips on Lake Maracaibo and festive activities in the city of Maracaibo. The festivities are marked by musical genres such as gaita and traditional dances such as the "Danza de las Cintas", in which dancers wave colourful ribbons.

Venezuela's traditional festivals and carnival celebrations not only provide entertainment and a sense of community, but are also a platform for cultural expression and identity. They connect people from different ethnic and social backgrounds and promote the preservation and transmission of traditional practices from generation to generation.

Handicrafts and local handicrafts

Handicrafts and local handicrafts play an important role in Venezuela and are an expression of the country's rich cultural diversity and traditions. A standout feature of Venezuelan handicrafts is its versatility and the use of local materials as well as traditional techniques that are often passed down through generations.

In the rural areas of Venezuela, traditional crafts such as weaving, pottery, basket weaving and wood carving are cultivated. Each region has its own distinctive styles and patterns that serve both practical and decorative purposes. For example, the production of hamacas, traditional hanging beds made of cotton or agave fibers, is an art form that is particularly practiced in the coastal areas and in the Andes.

Another well-known craft is the production of ceramics, which are used for everyday use as well as for religious and cultural purposes. Of particular note are the pottery from Lara State, known for its colorful designs and use of local clays.

Venezuela's indigenous people, especially the Warao people in the state of Delta Amacuro, are known for their intricately crafted baskets made of palm leaves, which are not only practical but also an important cultural heritage. These baskets are often decorated with traditional patterns that depict stories and symbols of indigenous culture.

Venezuela's artistic tradition also includes the production of hand-woven textiles, often dyed with natural dyes derived from plants, roots, and insects. These textiles are often worn during traditional festivals and ceremonies and are an important expression of the cultural identity of indigenous peoples and rural communities.

Modern Venezuelan artisans often incorporate traditional techniques and motifs into contemporary designs, resulting in a vibrant art scene that blends local craftsmanship with modern crafts. This is evident in the production of jewelry, leather goods, handmade furniture and decorative items, which are presented both at local markets and international fairs and exhibitions.

The promotion and preservation of Venezuelan handicrafts is of great importance, as it not only provides economic opportunities for the artisans, but also contributes to strengthening the country's cultural identity and heritage. Initiatives to train young artisans and create markets for traditional handicrafts help to keep this precious tradition alive and make it accessible to future generations.

Folklore and folk customs

Folklore and folk customs are at the heart of Venezuela's cultural identity and reflect the diversity and traditions of the different ethnic groups that populate the country. These customs are deeply rooted in the history and daily lives of the people and play an important role in festivals, ceremonies and in the social cohesion of the communities.

A central element of Venezuelan folklore is the numerous music and dance traditions, which vary regionally. For example, the Gaita, a musical genre from Zulia, is well known, which is played during the festival in honor of the Virgen de Chiquinquirá and is often accompanied by sung lyrics that tell local stories and legends. Equally characteristic is the joropo, a traditional dance from the Llanos that is characterized by a fast rhythm and acrobatic steps that reflect the agricultural activities of the region.

Religious festivals also play an important role in Venezuelan folklore. The festival in honor of the Virgen de la Candelaria in Mérida attracts believers and pilgrims from all over Venezuela who participate in processions and perform traditional dances that reflect the spiritual heritage of the region. In the coastal regions, festivals are held to honour the patron saints of fishermen, and in the Andes, rituals are practiced to worship mountain deities.

The folklore of Venezuela also includes a variety of myths, legends, and oral traditions that are often passed down from generation to generation. These stories tell of heroes, ghosts and natural phenomena and convey moral lessons and cultural values. An example of this is the legend of María Lionza, a mythological figure revered in Venezuelan popular religion and considered the protector of nature and indigenous peoples.

In addition to religious and musical traditions, culinary customs also play an important role in Venezuelan folklore. Traditional dishes such as arepas, hallacas and cachapas are not only food, but also symbols of cultural identity served at festivals and celebrations. These dishes connect people and serve as an expression of togetherness and Venezuela's cultural heritage.

The preservation and cultivation of Venezuela's folklore and folk customs is crucial for the preservation of the country's cultural diversity and identity. Initiatives to promote traditional crafts, music and dance help to preserve these rich cultural treasures and make them accessible to future generations. Folklore is thus not only an expression of the past, but also a living force in today's Venezuela, bringing communities together and strengthening the country's cultural heritage.

Sports enthusiasm and national heroes

The enthusiasm for sports in Venezuela is deeply rooted and plays a significant role in the country's national consciousness. Football is undoubtedly the most popular sport, and the Venezuelan national football team has become a symbol of national identity over the years. Fans passionately support their teams, both in domestic leagues and international competitions.

In addition to football, baseball and basketball are also very popular. Baseball has a long tradition in Venezuela and many players are internationally successful, especially in Major League Baseball (MLB) in the United States. Players like Miguel Cabrera and Félix Hernández are national heroes and are revered for their performances on and off the pitch.

Boxing also has a loyal fan base in Venezuela, and the country has produced several successful professional boxers who are internationally renowned. Boxing is a source of inspiration and pride for many Venezuelans.

In addition to traditional sports, there is also a growing enthusiasm for other disciplines such as athletics, swimming and cycling. Venezuelan athletes have achieved success in these areas in international competitions and are helping to represent the country on the global stage.

Support for sports in Venezuela is evident not only at the professional level, but also in the wide participation in amateur sports and in the development of sports programs for the youth. Sports clubs and schools promote sporting activity and provide a platform for young talents to develop and improve their skills.

National heroes in Venezuelan sports are known not only for their sporting achievements, but also for their commitment to social projects and their role as role models for the youth. Athletes like Yulimar Rojas, an outstanding track and field athlete and Olympic champion in the triple jump, are symbols of perseverance, determination and success.

The enthusiasm for sports in Venezuela is also reflected in the organization of major sporting events, such as the Copa América in soccer or the Serie del Caribe in baseball. These events not only bring fans together, but also strengthen the country's national pride and cultural identity.

Despite sporting challenges, such as financial constraints and infrastructure issues, the passion for sports remains strong in Venezuela and inspires generations of athletes and fans alike. The future of Venezuelan sports lies in nurturing talent and creating opportunities for young athletes to pursue their dreams and continue the legacy of sport in the country.

Tourism and travel advice

Tourism in Venezuela offers a variety of attractions and challenges for visitors from all over the world. The country is known for its natural beauty, from the Caribbean beaches to the majestic Andes Mountains and the Amazon rainforest. Angel Falls, the world's tallest waterfall, attracts adventure seekers who want to experience the unspoiled nature of Canaima National Park.

The Caribbean coast of Venezuela beckons with white sandy beaches and turquoise blue waters, ideal for sunbathing and water sports. The Los Roques archipelago is a paradise for divers and snorkelers who want to explore the rich underwater world. Puerto La Cruz and the coastal town of Margarita also offer prime beach resorts and historical attractions for visitors.

The Andean region of Venezuela is a mecca for trekking enthusiasts and nature lovers who want to explore the region's spectacular scenery and traditional villages. Mérida, the gateway to the Andes, offers not only breathtaking views, but also the opportunity to experience the culture and history of the region.

Historic cities such as Caracas, Ciudad Bolívar, and Maracaibo offer glimpses of Venezuela's colonial past and are home to architectural gems and cultural treasures. Tourists can visit museums, art galleries, and historic structures to learn about the country's rich history and heritage.

However, Venezuela is not without its challenges for travelers. The political and economic situation has led to social unrest and security problems, especially in urban areas. Travelers should check the latest travel advisories and take precautions to ensure their safety.

Traveling within Venezuela often requires flexibility and patience, as infrastructure and public services are not always reliable. It is recommended to use local tour operators and pay attention to up-to-date information on road conditions and transport options.

Despite the challenges, Venezuela offers adventurers and nature lovers a unique and fascinating travel experience. The diversity of landscapes, rich culture, and warm hospitality of the people make the country a worthwhile destination for explorers and adventurers who want to experience the world off the beaten track.

Future prospects for Venezuela

The future prospects for Venezuela face a number of challenges and opportunities that could shape the country's destiny. The economic situation remains unstable, marked by severe hyperinflation and a decline in oil production, which once formed the backbone of the Venezuelan economy. Reliance on oil exports has made the country vulnerable to international market fluctuations and complicated efforts at economic diversification and sustainable development.

Politically, Venezuela continues to experience tensions and polarization between different political camps. The ongoing political crises have led to social unrest and an exodus of skilled workers, which has affected the country's regeneration and stability. International sanctions and the lack of political agreement have exacerbated the situation and contributed to Venezuela's isolation on the global stage.

Inequalities and challenges persist in the country's social structure, especially in the areas of education, health care, and social security. Public services are inadequate in many places, which has led to a decline in quality of life and social mobility. Despite these challenges, there are efforts at the local level to improve social and economic conditions and strengthen communities.

Environmental issues such as deforestation, water pollution, and the effects of climate change also pose a serious threat to Venezuela's future. The government and international organizations are working on projects to protect natural resources and the environment, but implementation often remains a challenge.

Despite these challenges, there is potential for positive developments in Venezuela. The country's rich natural diversity offers opportunities for sustainable tourism and environmental protection projects. Venezuela's young population brings with it great potential for innovation and economic renewal, especially in areas such as technology and renewable energy.

The international community has an important role to play in supporting Venezuela on its path to stability and prosperity. Humanitarian aid, development cooperation and diplomatic efforts are crucial to address the crisis and promote long-term solutions to the country's economic, political and social challenges.

Venezuela's future depends on a variety of factors, including political developments, economic reforms, and the strengthening of social infrastructure. The ability to address these challenges and seize opportunities will be critical to shaping a stable and prosperous future for the Venezuelan people and their generations to come.

Closing remarks

The concluding word of this book on Venezuela offers a look back at the comprehensive presentation of this fascinating country, which inspires and moves at the same time with its diversity of landscapes, cultures and challenges. From the majestic Andes in the west to the vast plains of the Orinoco in the east, Venezuela presents a unique natural beauty characterized by its rich biodiversity and variety of ecosystems.

Historically, Venezuela has undergone a complex evolution, from pre-Columbian cultures to the colonial era to independence and the challenges of the 20th century. The political upheavals and economic challenges have shaped the country and shaped its current situation.

Venezuela's social structure reflects the diversity of its population, including indigenous communities, Afro-Venezuelan traditions, and a rich cultural heritage. The challenges in education and health care are real, as are the efforts to achieve social equality and economic stability.

Venezuela's cultural scene is characterized by a vibrant music and dance tradition, a thriving literary scene, and a rich heritage of handicrafts and folk customs. The carnival and traditional festivals are an expression of this cultural vitality and celebrate the cultural identity of the country.

The future of Venezuela faces challenges, but also potential. The development of sustainable tourism projects and the protection of natural resources could pave the way to sustainable economic development. Strengthening social infrastructure and promoting political stability are crucial for the well-being of the Venezuelan people.

Overall, Venezuela is a country of contrasts and opportunities. Hope rests on the ability of Venezuelan society to jointly address challenges and bring about positive change. May this book help to spark a deeper understanding and interest in this fascinating country and contribute to the discussion about its future.

Made in the USA
Coppell, TX
13 April 2025

48243000R00066